Exile

Winner of the
United States Award
of the International Poetry Forum
1974

Exile

❧

THOMAS
RABBITT

UNIVERSITY OF PITTSBURGH PRESS

Library of Congress Cataloging in Publication Data

Rabbitt, Thomas, birth date
  Exile.

(Pitt poetry series)
Poems.
I. Title.
PS3568.A22E9   811'.5'4   74–17527
ISBN 0–8229–3292–X
ISBN 0–8229–5256–4 pbk.

Some of the poems in this book appeared originally in *Black Warrior Review* and *Shenandoah,* and are reprinted with the permission of the editors.

for Marcel Smith

Contents

PART TWO: *Spring*

PART THREE: *Summer*

PART FOUR: *Fall*

Acknowledgments

The author is grateful for permission to use the following material:

Three lines from W. H. Auden, "Musée des Beaux Arts." From *Collected Shorter Poems, 1927–1957* by W. H. Auden, published by Random House, Inc. Copyright 1940 and renewed 1968 by W. H. Auden.

One line from John Berryman, "Henry's Confession." From *The Dream Songs* © 1969 by John Berryman. Used by permission of Farrar, Straus & Giroux, Inc.

Two lines from John Berryman, "Homage to Mistress Bradstreet." From *Homage to Mistress Bradstreet and Other Poems* © 1956, 1968 by John Berryman. Used by permission of Farrar, Straus & Giroux, Inc.

One line from Johnny Cash, "Folsom Prison Blues." Copyright © by Hilo Music, Inc.

Four lines from T. S. Eliot, "The Waste Land." From *Collected Poems, 1909–1962* by T. S. Eliot, copyright 1936 by Harcourt Brace Jovanovich, Inc., copyright © 1963, 1964, by T. S. Eliot. Reprinted by permission of Harcourt Brace Jovanovich, Inc. Published in England by Faber and Faber Ltd, London, and used by permission.

Two lines from Steve Goodman, "City of New Orleans." Copyright © 1971, Buddah Music, Inc., and Turnpike Tom Music. Used by permission.

Two lines from June Hershey and Don Swander, "Deep in the Heart of Texas." Copyright 1941, Melody Lane Publications, Inc. Copyright renewed, Melody Lane Publications, Inc. Used by permission.

Two lines from Richard Hugo, "The Lady in Kicking Horse Reservoir." From *The Lady in Kicking Horse Reservoir* by Richard Hugo. W. W. Norton & Company, Inc., New York, N.Y. Copyright © 1973 by Richard Hugo.

Two lines from Donald Justice, "To the Hawks." Copyright © 1966 by Donald Justice. Reprinted from *Night Light* by Donald Justice, by permission of Wesleyan University Press. "To the Hawks" first appeared in *Poetry*.

PART ONE: *Winter*

EXILE

i.

"He should anchor the abstraction."
"That's it—to anger *the abstraction . . . "*

—Theodore Roethke

You are breaking down the let house into all
its abstractions, the can idling on the kitchen floor,
the dog sucking the rug.
Each dark follower in this interim of rooms arranges
to be dead, four score and ten, and twenty, the 100th door
is it open, do it be cut?
Forests loom in the woodwork, the oak opening a fistful.
Grain for African deer, for precious small rats in the wall.
The parlor is falling! *Gloriosa tarmes.* The beast
is feminine, ranges
through the humus and the wishful rock.
You are breaking down this wall for a translation.
Your hand is subtle how you parse
everything from most forest to least:
flesh is a structure you think bound to spit out.

EXILE

ii.

They came down the aisle, fucking dog style,
while the orchestra played Kilmer's Trees.

—from a limerick

Their trees refuse to winter, and drop
in a slow burn across the land, the strafe of ash
and a smell remain.
The women who are safe come out,
gather in heaps, retrench. The custom is called
catching, something you do
with others to be like them, to eat, as they do,
to watch for your men as they fall among the leaves.
You go with them to gather us up for the fire.
The burn wards off rain and,
in these wet months, keeps things parched, safe,
your child away from desire, the house warm,
the ingredients for dry bread—flour and salt—loose
in the sieve. You fill sackcloth with ashes, no waste,
and make our bed comfortable from foot to top.

EXILE

iii.
Those we captured we left behind;
those that escaped us we carried home.

—Homer's riddle

Lately the weather has been vermin, it falls,
scratching all of us instead; and it left the foundations
rotting in the ground. Of course we needed them
for the better life, for the maid and her boy,
for Christmas. The weather is lousy.
You have African sensations, the cats have fleas.
And the walls too. Nothing rids us of them,
this common itch to be out and in. Mother told you:
marriage and career make strange troubles follow, and she
got all the 18th C. for proof.
The thing is different now; each wheeze, one bite—
these things fear *us*. We are like elephants,
we live in trees, we warn the weather by scratching at it
through the roof and door. And the birds, bless them,
who feed from the cracks in our skin.

EXILE

iv.

A German ambassador once told me he cdn't bear St. Paul
he was, he said, so hard on fornication.

—Ezra Pound

I can always be too hard on the saints, they're in it
with us, like the conscientious blind man who wants not
to pee on toilet seats. And our hostess who claims
never you mind.
I mind, and you also, for the cleaning up to be done
in the foreign places which surround us.
The tiles in a rest room, the odd birds, even the cast of a road
—all of it shames.
So you ask: do you blame the house builder?—he begins it;
or the renter who, at the end, is caught
under the shedding paint and a load of weekend guests come to see
how he manages the art of out?
Never. One writes letters, quotes the Latin and the big fuss;
and cites my wife for instance; and Saint Paul; and
whoever else, among the rest, helped make life rum.

EXILE

The mouth of the world
Grows round with the sound.

—Donald Justice

What with the railroads dead and the buses
filled with blacks and going declassé
timetables are harder to read for the prices, downs, ups.
Like Dante's charts, or Hugo's, the boldface is better: say
Niente per voi or, this is good for wrapping butter.
We know the sounds of guns; at Christmas we think
butter sounds like hip pockets going slack.
Yes, it is coming and the planes are fat
with the sweat and bloat of those who see they may die
just going back for a holiday. Best not to leave.
Darling wife, if we stay and are careful with our cups
the war will pass over the house like a great bird
with a bellyful of vacationers.
Each day we can watch the paper boy wonder why
instead of a wreath you have tacked a new list to the door.

EXILE

vi.

If *life is a handkerchief sandwich* . . .

—John Berryman

The first tacked to the door: a list of casualties who crawled
between the floorboards and the Persian rugs.
They keep us dancing. My darling, yesterday you said that
these others would keep out, or you'd kill them all.
So today—*noli nos tangere*—your enemies you serve us,
carpet sandwiches with a spread I say are crushed Eyetalian bugs.
With this whole whorl of domestic troubles you can laugh?
And you must, I guess, each time I sit at table, pass your hat
through the kitchen, you under it like a wind, like eggs
and chickens, like a Jewish question. So you say: fuss!
Ain't I got everything to do? Your dinners are a two-horse race
and I make it in next to last. You make second. Oh, hope,
on long meals who ends up between? Topside the dregs
are butter for the morning toast; for supper you serve mold,
flat enemies fearing a *pas de dieu* in our open-faced dance.

8

EXILE

vii.

After that alien, point-blank, green and actual Guatemala.

—Wallace Stevens

This much is certain: down here one gets a pun
for the peso, one way to spend an Xmas, all
the kiddies talking Spic, in Spanish, in runs
and trills like green birds.
Oh darling are you moulting after Mayan studs?
What will the paper boy say when you call
from Puerto Barrios to cancel out the *Tuscaloosa News?*
Ees long deestanz calling Ali Bama—egzepdt charge?
Always this fussing after that alien word
and the shot in the head in the dark obvious room.
You return to the hotel: Pedro Alvarado, you say, as large
as life, *Conquistador*, I met him on the beach
dead these last four centuries. You'll roam
anywhere, won't you? On your back, in alleys, pews,
Ultimate Foreigner, you are, the vacationing dove of peace.

EXILE

viii.
The holly has a berry as red as the blood . . .

—from a carol

Foetus navidad, dear, under the mistletoe and holly
with berries swimmingly out of busted veins, the cells
separate the while you sleep in your lonely bones
your flesh unlovely and your skin on the beach calls
to be burned. What rotten luck
your pregnancy takes, the shape of a wen, I see,
red lines and white growth on your cheek
like a third eye.
Foolish of you to suggest that I do Rome
and you would lay confined in Acapulco
under the gooseberry eye of the sun, no way to spend
the Little Christmas, each suffering the feast
on different continents. The crowd is shouting:
Bulla! Bulla! and from his balcony His Holiness just said
your wife, sir, has managed to miscarry one child thrice.

EXILE

ix.
I like to see it lap the miles . . .

—Emily Dickinson

So spouse it has a long tongue, this adventure, and probes
to the core of my problem. You too have friends?
To lick each voyage dry?—*et haec*
olim meminisse iuvabit—Think! of my walls and groves,
of things fallen on their knees at the rail,
Father begging for burial. Both closed ends
sail happy into their perspective, a renaissance like
the narrowing mouths of my journey forced to say, "Ah!"
Dear spouse I write to tell you someone
is dragging by the countryside this window at a terrible rate.
And, *vulva et pudendum*, the trainman gave me leave
to sit on the tip of the tongue.
It's coruscated, a jewel box, this gate
up through this American Adventure, oh wife. I say live,
and why not? Like me, to be down at the mouth and hung.

EXILE

x.

Some people are men and some people are women.
They're made that way so they can dance together.

—Lucille Ball

Lucy arrived yesterday, on the skids, she said.
We all in this together, on a down rail. It do bode ill—
her words. On your map, she says, for no good reason,
south is down and hell is underneath.
She's a little devil, can change her sex, a cute fabric
disorderly like the curtains or the skinny road outside,
from the R.R. Station to the bed.
Fire twits the lower region, below her belly button,
a nice furnace, an appetite for people and the will
to change into anyone. On inclination.
The South's too warm, she says, and they tell lies, spread-
legged in the streets, line each room in my house o'call.
They're like rugs in a tiger cage. She tanned their hides
and promised to eat them up, chain, cock, and ball,
and the why her lovers smell so bad is that they're dead.

EXILE

xi.
What you get married for if you don't want children?
HURRY UP PLEASE ITS TIME

—T. S. Eliot

It's 1492 and the planet chucks its gut.
The wedges out like an orange, this marriage, a *telos*.
So, Sweetie, it comes to this,
the big divorce, the silver yours, our dear tomorrows
spent rerolling paper, getting glue into the pot.
SAVE! SAVE! Columbus is in chains and his Indios.
He sailed too far. The planet and house list.
One explorer called me Hatchet-over-Baby-Belly,
called you Dull-Wit-under-each-and-every-Pain.
Solomon and Jewish Mother, and of the three
Child-to-be-Split-like-Orange-Earth peeps out, *the world*
ain't flat, is flat, be generous. Like the Pope's wrist:
one flick and the New World was for Portugal and Spain.
On this side of the corpse the hair is straight, on this curled.
The choice tickles the Prelate and the Queen.

EXILE

xii.
All for number one. Cute as a shithouse rat.
Hundred to five.

—James Joyce

Do you understand the odds against the Jews, success,
marriage, divorce or the price of meat
going down? Dear lady, next time you go
ad altare dei, go on your hands and knees like a rat
rutting under the outhouse where the light is best
and you can get food sifted through the floorboards.
Blood- or organ-meats depending so
on who plays cat, law- and manna-giver.
It was you who said: this relationship must end,
an unhealthy thing, here away from all our friends,
and based on sex. So you were bored.
Incompatibility: kidneys are his food, mine is chops,
Your Honor, and besides I conclude he has no
INNER RESOURCES and says I fuck like liver
and for that I want the baby, the silver and the chairs.

EXILE

xiii.
Get thee to a nunnery . . . for wise men know
well enough what monsters you make of them.

—Shakespeare

O, for the good old days and the religious wars,
blood in the byways, tumbrils packed with meaty
battle beautiful, joined, enlarging
like blood turning in and out of the convent doors.
These raped nuns, see how they run.
Easter is coming, the lamb is getting fat
and you women take this thing, ah,
too serious, as at the dance you, with GREETINGS:
I'm off to be a nun in Halifax.
Don't! you say, it's Lent, Nova Scotia's not much fun.
Nolo facere novus and, had I wished to, I
could've married a mustachioed sister in a blue serge suit.
The storm's come. The dams of your convent tremble while
Mother Superior says, grow Dutch, little boy,
give us the finger, or tongue, to the very root.

15

xiv.
Like a long-legged fly upon the stream
Her mind moves upon silence.

Sweetheart, the dog rooting in the humus smel
from where you hide deep in your puddle.
You shouldn't run away. The children came in
to see you naked, to ask how much you'll take
for a peek, that old eternal through the veil.
O temperate maiden, seasonal shellfish, sho
Sweets for the sweetest and coals, hot coals,
You see, kiddies, her own mama expected he
and end chewing her tongue.
The bruise on her baby's head grew lurid lik
and she went balmy, said the child had a ta
and dropped him no less than twice.
It's Ash Wednesday, darling. You must m
Time for your plenary self-indulgence, *ca*
put your lips to this. Kids, what's coming

xv.
The
into

Your
I stoo
she ca
where
is mad
throug
her on
Oh Sir,
lest the
and tha
They c
hunted
with th
she pro
They se

EXILE

illway's open and you spill out
eather, lover down the bright canal . . .

—Richard Hugo

Ionor, she upped the flagpole each morning at eight.
to and saluted her, waving, afraid of the spell
weave with names: *Tuscaloosa, Alabama*
the elephants come to die, and the *Black Warrior*
of Negroes and new brides in a rush over the spillway
the gate she left open and the tusky scrub bulls,
he pole waving them on, excited, to make her on a dare.
she was fearful sore and I was scared
child be caught up in the madness, tra-la,
prize nose of his give over the clue.
me to me at night, alewives from the Klan,
ast the door, upstairs to the bed for the sheets
holes and stains. So, Your Eminence, for Lent
ised to give up patriotism and large pets.
it anyway; I have to sleep with things smelling burnt.

PART TWO: *Spring*

EXILE

xvi.
The race is not always to the swift.

—a silly old saw

The gimpy black man, dear, wiped our table once too often,
it made you drool with spring, the thought of his peg
and other sacrifices, clammy flesh, tabletops spread
with butter and meat. You say that butter sounds like
turtles in migration over the roadway crushed, softened,
you, delighted. See how they run, you said,
out of their shells at the edges, tureens of blood and legs.
Reach me that bag of worms, this is one helluva flood.
In times of trouble you run for the dikes;
you call them pecker-crafts, the dead fish floating
tripe white and loverlike, all your men in the one bath.
The black waiter is coming with your seventh glass of water
and you want, oh so much, to touch his wood
at the joint. Dear girl, he limps to disaster,
your dark fish, hooked on a worm and ready for loading.

EXILE

xvii.
In their jars the snail-nosed babies moon and glow.
He hands her the cut-out heart like a cracked heirloom.

—Sylvia Plath

Flora (Floribunda), Flora Carsick, *nomen*, you bloom
inside us and feed on bags of air.
My wife's breathing distracts you, calls to mind
conspiracies and the universal Esperanzas
of the dull. Crabby Moribunda, Unborn Urchin,
Certificates all right, p.o.e. Boston, rented rooms
over the grocer's, the butcher's, shameless glee at the counters
over the blood meats. You stuffed a lung with greens.
Darling thinks you are an angel, seasonal and kind.
You are another lunar pregnancy, that old-time Easter dare
that she will tack me up, or I her,
that one from the wood and the meat will be weaned
like Jesus Christ, pockets full of cancer
and all the while there is our skin as old as raisins.
In a corner the altar jar and a nosegay of bones.

EXILE

xviii.
The only man in the world who ever made an active
attempt to seduce me was a parakeet lover.*

—Marcel Smith

My wife enjoys the restaurateur who puts mushrooms
on canaries, those arrangements of love.
I for one love grated Romano on my son.
Senatus Populusque Romano delivers.
Free. My wife always thinks to charge less, to cost
so little that she disappears and each of the children
follows her like a balloon unblowing itself.
Birth should always be clear: small dots
are eaten by the larger, fry by fish, my son
(in the maudlin pie) by the old king, all shove
by push, my wife who eats garnished hearts and livers
and, on Ember days, the feathers, the actual pelf
of an adulterous canary. Lent is a cauldron
of feathers, when for grief the sweet angels moult
and all the cages open into rooms.

**His parakeet was named Oscar.*

EXILE

xix.
Quite unexpectedly as Vasserot . . .

—Archibald MacLeish

Simultaneously the one-armed man rolls himself
a cigarette and picks your nose.
Lambkin, I know you always cuddle too close
to This World's stumps and scars, finding a wealth
of sin and comfort (some call it *sex*) in the lamed
or leprous. You strike a match, he smokes his finger.
It is Rose Sunday, the middle of Lent, when things
give way a little and the bars are open late.
Yes, my lamb, we all want our pores tamed,
each hole opened wider and the pain to linger
where it has no right. The drum is fainting,
Easter in Alabama hangs by a toe.
You, lamb, with all the organs in you, yell, fainting:
let go! let go! The one-armed man makes your bell ring
and I watch while inside you Jocko's stump grows.

EXILE

XX.

Arms with hands grasping seek to clutch at the prows.
Bodies thrown recklessly in the way are cut aside.
—William Carlos Williams

This here Black Warrior runs blood. A social guilt
intrudes, ruins my cotton Woolworth orientals because
you and your rubber baby let the tub go
two weeks. Let me say it's filled.
Liz called her baby John, *Giovanni Battista,*
after *La Strega,* our omnivorous Alabama mother.
Through our living room, swimming on their laws,
the Baptists come to take him to the river.
Cleo: that head, my lord? On the dark waters the barges
come and go carrying the people who know
how to be saints—rubadubdub—the butcher, baker, stick maker
on the banks of Chief Tuskaloosa, by the blood brown water.
Our L. watches J. baptize these whom the Spirit filled.
My rugs can be saved when the water withdraws
if like saints they are hung on a line to claw the wind.

EXILE

xxi.

You cannot sit on bayonets,
Nor can you eat among the dead.

—Delmore Schwartz

He spit into her left ear and she could listen again
to snow fall south. The mayor called it a miracle
and let the key to the city into her brain.
Everyone came for the ceremony, came in heavenwear,
and were arrayed right to left, Baptist Church
to Anglican to (*sotto voce*) Jew.
It was a good day for medical
wonders, a Choose-day, so on order from the Warner
Studios all the Gulf potentates bent over to belch.
Like the judging jaysus on the last, best riding cloud
prosperity rounded the corner in smoke
smelling of sausage and pensions and merds. I waved
used palms and a white she-ass with colt.
One university president came out of the 19th C. daze,
stars played bars, there was no containing the crowd.

EXILE

xxii.
Howdy, Mister Dillon!

—Chester

When is an odor not an odor? When it's a widow
ajar into the next world. The movie comes crawling
out of her. Mama Earth, resurrection is Roy Rogers
riding Dale Evans (sweet Buttermilk) from the rodeo
down the dotted white lines—between the rigors
of words and the hard death. Trigger, a Southerner, drawling:
Marse Roy, I'se a stallion, ain't she my turn
to ride you into the sonnets? They do endure.
Outside it's Easter; there are smells and messages:
lilies, placentas, white letters on black marquees beside
the churches. *Buy orchards. Take a ride*
with Christ to glory. It's the pain you abhor;
it and old films are sin's wages.
Bullet, the devildog, chases butterflies into the ferns
and Nellybelle, lamb of peace, overheats on the last late show.

EXILE

xxiii.
The ant's a centaur in his dragon world.
Pull down thy vanity . . .

—Ezra Pound

Here we go again loping into the green green grass
of Pentecost. They stand in black suits on the porch.
They are *Turmwachters* and are bent on saving us.
My wife's new list is up on the door and it includes
them among others: Mammals, Seven-Day Wonders, and a gross
of brush and button men. I say, am never rude,
in best Bostonian, we don't hold with no church.
They understand, flutter the pages of magazines, I
drop my dimes and the dog in the window barks.
Friends, we never eat, but hunger after whoever should die
here on the porch. They understand.
One says, now that Easter is over, you should embark
on the race to Hope. He drools over my crutch
and my wife, knowing the scrawled list is her hand,
small and tasty. Cat-licks, he says, hurt the worst.

EXILE

xxiv.
Said the waiter, don't shout and wave it about
or the others will all want one too.

—from a limerick

Friends, are you eating Custard now? Enjoying her less?
Does she come to bed with razors? Can the dog
roll his own and bury it along with your bones?
Has your maid nailed shut the clean rooms
and left you to live in the halls? Are you celibate?
My daughter's swollen like a puppy. Her brother's distressed.
We've all forgotten how to masticate.
Late spring is foremost laxative, and our smells bloom
under the dry pecans in the yard. Here we are lone
squatters over a cure. Darling, can you really love a Wog?
Near summer is when she finally accepts fat, death and a hex
on her bed. The maid carpets the foyer walls so thick
I can sleep in pile, hung so I can't toss.
My wife leaves it there. Squirrels desert the pecans, the ticks
drop off hungry. Each body hole is looked into loss.

EXILE

XXV.

Water? Fish fuck in water.

—attributed to W. C. Fields

Twelve Month's Mind Masses can drink up the money.
My wife and I celebrated Ascension Thursday and the debates
twixt Mr. Fields and Mr. McCarthy. No oblivion was ever better.
Satan is a woodpecker; any mannikin can be his bed and board.
My son sits with his father on his knee and calls
the world's only venerable drunk a bore.
Son: you're the kind of moron joke time deflates.
Father: the bus driver said, no more on, but on I pressed
until the bus was empty and I, alone, grew bitter.
Your mother was disgusted to the roots of her hair.
The glue grows soft, her teeth clack, and all
her wishes turn to splinters. *Dies irae*, will we float to the top?
What do you call a requiem for carved pine? Ash Wednesday? Fire?
It's a fair view of descent: each father stops
on his son's knee when his son's mouth gets tired.

xxvi.

What of that terrible lightness, ephemeral brightness—
The Butterfly-pestilence ending the race of Man?

—Edith Sitwell

It's the ear mites who like old songs in summer made you
think of that, a study, deep as a trench
from the Great War. In your one eye the Kaiser's on parade.
You hum, *Over There*, if only, you say, it was August, 1914.
The war is over, Rational Free Europe is playing *Lily Marlene*,
and a Cooperative for American Remittances to Everywhere has sent
a few good souls into the future to look for you.
Things, you say, tend to get smaller and hard to find.
But you'll take anything, a mite or louse, on trade
for now, so long as it digs in.
Lice suck. Everything is sex. To have summer you remember pain,
lie abed, and think hard of the bees coming in to bomb.
Melliferarum apium. The crash was fatal. The hum
in your ears is as long
as the coming needle I have to use to cure your song.

PART THREE: *Summer*

EXILE

xxvii.

. . . it passes the wretched trap whelming and I am me
drencht & powerful, I did it with my body!

—John Berryman

That simperer my husband lives too long, I love him still
though he would bring one and another strange thing
into my house. A statue of Tecumseh, one male Negro
lame in the nether leg, the elephants with bad teeth
and two horses made the stairs clatter, our brass bed ring
like the coronation scene from *Boris Godunov*.
The racket could kill lice. I had enough to steel
against, and more, the expectation of a low
opinion from the neighbors when the floors should fall.
For we had termites, we have them still.
Everyone here has bugs, though at home we are loathe
to advertise it. They're *his* pets, all, even the geese
you can hear squawking at midnight, him shoving his own *paté*.
If he reaches for *me*, I hear the baby cry. I cry also;
think of the neighbors, what they think, what they must say.

EXILE

xxviii.
*Those who restrain desire do so because
theirs is weak enough to be restrained.*

—William Blake

Last month he married off himself to red clay dust
and horses and the mouth-watering legislation for draft beer.
He watches trees. It's all the same, he says, how they
predict and then condemn the weather. I hate him then,
when he goes drunk and says he's come to grips with genders,
plagues and conjugations. Sir, my marriage must
be in trouble, but for the trees I could see a way
to the end. He reads wood grain and leaves and I fear
more than anything he might forget himself there.
I have, he said, *a finger on this county's pulse and a nostril
up her ass*. There are things a lady must not say
though she lie back and itch for his love. I can remember
his son in pounds and ounces, his thing in fractions of an inch.
I wait, like him, for that final, flat wind on the door.
I know you can never believe he married a loose bitch.

EXILE

xxix.
I suspect this is a nice enough town
once it snows,
but what do you do with your hands?

—Elizabeth Libbey

He's out again. Drink to his one American activity.
Split my girdle in the middle so the electric death
I desire can up me like a lover.
I'll give their secrets. Christie is in the lounge, before her
it was Red Lucy, and before her I had no idea of the breadth
of the keyboard. Am I still cunning?
If I tell you how he prays for snow, like a barometer
his penis in August keyed to occasional lows, his eyes
as cold as olives,—my flesh was my dowry—think
of me as a kind woman who kneels on her hands.
At the execution he'll give me up like
a bad reason, like a reformed queer gives up boys, like
the South has given up its snowmen. Take my wedding band;
gold is a bad conductor. My girdle feels like liver.
Tragic: snow or adultery here, either would be funny.

EXILE

XXX.

The deep-mouthed bloodhound's heavy bay
Resounded up the rocky way . . .

—Sir Walter Scott

That sot each night will drink his fill and leave me home to kill
the hours swatting bats out of the drapes. The nights are hot,
and the sheets, everything heavy with sweat, too much
for a Yankee Lady to bear. He reels in like Catfish, like as not
reeking of beer, his horses and dreams of the blond-wigged doll
plays piano, all coos and bills, for the drivers in the hotel bar.
Your Honor, he whistles show tunes in his sleep
and smells of stable muck and the hussy's Shalimar.
What's a girl to do? I'm married to the bats, and not the lush
humming *Oklahoma* in that obscene cotton slip
he calls a nightshirt. He sprays deodorants up the chimney,
rose or azalea, says the bats'll leave, *anti-flora, que sera, sera,*
and if they don't, well, fuck 'em. Your Honor, he thinks I have.
There's more to be considered. It's not just me.
I have an infant son who likes the bats and whistles *April Love.*

EXILE

xxxi.
Watch out! You'll step on the Brain's toes, Fingers.

—Lucille Ball

Dear Mama, yesterday I had a letter from him signed, the Brain.
My darling wife, he began, I'm off west, a young man
to California with Horace Greeley and Lucille.
Send beer.
Just like that, on a line all by itself. And then: *if thou fain*
wdst sell my body for the rent, thou cdst live a pretty while.
I've called. The hospital wants them free and clear,
and he, I'm afraid, is foggy thru and thru, although
properly pickled. But that's no selling point.
He wrote more: from here the Rockies rise above the plain
like Lucy's teeth from her red-red lip. He did say lip.
Mama, I found him this morning down in the coal bin, a pint
empty in one hand, and his pants were gone—to Frisco, on the trip
with Horace, I suppose. You know how I must feel:
he had no shoes and there was lipstick on his left great toe.

EXILE

xxxii.

As from a green tin coffin, so a woman's head
Emerges slowly—her dark hair heavily oiled—

—Arthur Rimbaud

Summer by the pool is one roll of fat after another
slipping over the waistband of my bikini.
Teach the boy to swim, he says. The boy's an infant,
he swims in diapers every time he pees. So I'm the mother
of a fish, I say, and he: you can be Mama Esther Williams
for all I care. The boy swims.
So here I am, the bellyroll o'erleaping the ruin of my pants
and I'd been on a diet. Not for him; for me,
lest that thing I felt was growing grow some more between
my legs and my knees could never touch.
Here we are—so many wives and children, and the thin young
who make me think I could kill him and be done
with growing fat and aging. O, for one touch
of that boy's thigh, and it could leave a tattoo and I'd be seen
for what I am, slim and childless and free.

EXILE

xxxiii.
*Faraway hands are folded and folded
or pick at the threads in the lap of blackness . . . .*

—George Starbuck

While he rides trains I take planes and spite him
because I live. I've saved each policy, the kind you buy
like soft drinks at the airport. In one I named the Pope.
My husband never understood that kind of humor.
It's time: I want to leave for Christmas in July,
fly from Boston to the Cape in time to roar
through Falmouth Heights and see Santa, young, brown and slim,
stuffing the silk stockings of older ladies at the Oak Crest Inn.
From the cellar my husband says it's good to live with hope,
and to pray, and to trust finally enough to take a plane.
Kind feelings, he says, should be bottled like a spray so
you can play godmother against the dark. This is good snow
to insure against an early spring; this is pain—
sure against moralists and the sins they say they fear.

EXILE

xxxiv.
Slept at night in a dog kennel
But nobody chained him up.

—Dylan Thomas

The neighbors have our fleas. The wives came today,
a welcome wagonful, nine months too late and
for the first time close enough to spit.
Hubby was home, trapped by a bat I'd let into his study.
He's helpless with a hangover. Mrs. Eubanks smiled, began:
Ma'am, we know you through your dogs and I see your husband
out feeding the geese. You have so many cats—
it was then the baby cried—but we think you must be lonely.
We've never seen you shopping or at church.
I smiled. Mrs. Snider lifted up her skirt and scratched her knee.
The dog oozed behind the couch. I could hear a noise
from the study. They agreed the Baptist minister was nice.
I said: we're pantheists. Mrs. Eubanks dabbed at her crotch.
The dog looked up and hubby yelled, *we worship bats!*
Like Leda's swan, the thing itself was a test of poise.

EXILE

The sage in bloom is like perfume
Deep in the heart of Texas.

—from the song

I know some French and a little German, *c'est wahr,*
nur ein peut-être, too much for a woman, he'd say,
but it does me better than his Greek, our men, men,
deep in their abstractions, his *telos,* he dreams of war
between the ceiling and the floor, the ideal wall.
He's as mercurial as a verb: if I can't take you
to the Riviera, how about Austin?
I've got a ride. It's all the same: the Gulf or middle-earth
when you work his way.
C'est comme ça le biscuit s'emiet, he's heading for a fall—
Écrase-toi la banane. Frohliche Weinachten!
It's for him I bought the German boots and learned to screw
in French: *Ah, donnez-moi la plume!* My ass
is telic. For a plate of spaghetti I'd give birth
in Italian, with a rattler and his horse we're off to Texas.

EXILE

xxxvi.

. . . if a woman showed her belly to the full moon after
she had done caught, it would be a gal.

—William Faulkner

The Fourth is popped and gone like a pimple, the salmon grew fat
I should know. We had peas, they call them English here.
There's Labor Day to wait for. That used to be the end
and we could sing a swan song for summer.
Even the time between my periods lasts longer. Like as not,
as they say, I'm pregnant, no visit, as they say, from my friend.
The moon's been full since winter, if you would call
the sky making too much water winter. I can't pass water,
and my husband passes up the bed is all
the proof I need. I keep my knees pressed together
till the blood thickens and, white as flesh, the girlmoon
pulls at the baby till she cries, *not here! not here!*
I've promised her Quebec. My husband will carry wood
and boil snow. My daughter will be born in French,
if at all, saying, *merci, ma mere, merci* I wasn't born too soon.

EXILE

xxxvii.
I'm the train they call the City of New Orleans.
I'll be gone 500 miles when the day is done.

—Steve Goodman

Over the spreading whiskey stain my drunken husband mourns.
He tries to explain: the why I use a bottle is
you get too drunk faster with a glass. I know what he means
to say is, sorry we're not leaving, I've got the rug to kiss.
I had the babies packed, inside and out, then he said we had to have
a truck for the books and animals.
I don't see why, if they love us, they can't follow
like a train. He could blow into his bottles.
So what if a page gets torn or one kitten is so slow
she can't keep up? So he says, it's easy for you to laugh
at the vicissitudes of travel, but the helpless beasts
are babes in arms and need each small care.
New Orleans is the wrong end of the line, but even that end recedes
from his tongue on the rug. I know. Next he treats
me to a drink, and I join him on my hands and knees.

EXILE

xxxviii.
They know that Hamlet and Lear are gay;
Gaiety transfiguring all that dread.

—William Butler Yeats

He's been up all night birthing cats, calls it queening
what the mother is when that first slick sac lets go.
The one that died he carried to the country, buried it
in foil under red dirt at the base of a pine tree
near his horses' barn. He took from the barn, or so
he says, a foundation block to keep the thing down.
There's hope left for him, or is he pruning
his nervous feathers? I'll never know.
Each after each funeral is all it is, and then he worried that
the thing would not be dead. He blamed me.
But who am I to listen like a bill collector at a corpse's mouth?
The sealed eyes looked wrong, not there, and the head was wrong.
I could've knocked, *are you there?* like they do
when the Pope dies. Thus, thus, to dig it up, to be sure, he's gone
all the way back, and he *will* be gay inside this other myth.

EXILE

Water, water, everywhere,
And all the boards did shrink; . . .

—Samuel Taylor Coleridge

Dear Mama, the weather feels like we're all living
underwater. I drown at bedtime and he's around
my neck like a tired swimmer giving
me instructions how to save him. Stroke, one,
two, three, stroke! dammit! Sometimes he'll say
don't bother. How can I bother? These dog days
I'm not even sure I'm pregnant, no kick, no sound,
as if the thing is treading water, learning all the tricks
from its father. *This is how to float on her bones, on her lungs.*
It's this climate makes him do it, plays those old tricks
on me instead of him. Today he says that he's
(oh!) in love again, this a cross-eyed girl who sells
pet supplies and gives him a new slant on things.
Mama, can she show him a way out, can she please
him, or swim a straight sidestroke without water wings?

PART FOUR: *Fall*

EXILE

xl.

I killed a man in Reno just to watch him die.

—Johnny Cash

I wish I'd done that, to mark what can't be bound:
this thin passage from above to down, out, like breathing
into his garden, disturbing the tomatoes, all leaf
and no fruit, or the squash that goes to ground
from yellow flowers with the rain into an orange rot.
As his wife I am conscious of things: the hard, brief
birthdays, his escape into vermin, like as not,
large murders in places called *small town*
and insignificant. While we are leaving,
while I am unleaving him, I can't be funny.
I'll need all my patient fingers to unglue his parts,
uproot his gardens, *paulo maiora canamus,* be an ark,
silly, to his precious vermin. It's easy for me.
Not Reno, not that line, but a trap like a truck
hidden for him under the bed, baited with the letter *fuck.*

EXILE

xli.

Every woman adores a Fascist,
The boot in the face, the brute
Brute heart of a brute like you.

—Sylvia Plath

He called me beautiful, without threat or provocation, said
my looks could deter a stone from the straits
of dalliance. Once I might've been. It's all to turn my head
from the purpose: Love is not enough, not Death,
not the songs that follow him through the foyer and the streets
to the choked, crabby bars. He said: it must be about
something, it's not enough to die, to breathe
and die. I whisper, *Love.* He says, *what?*
and *never mind* in the same breath and leaves for the streets.
What does he find there? Alabama roaches? Young boys
who live in their legs? Like milk and cream, the separated gut
and limb of my last lover, him? Before I was asleep
last night he tried to masturbate.
I know what it meant then to give my hands and head
in wedlock, liking what I could not bear to taste.

EXILE

xlii.
By and by the magician
Will put us all
Back in the box.

—Charles Simic

I call upon the Pope, Bishops and Martyrs, Sainted Virgins
and you, Honorable Judge, *mon semblable, mon homme*
to witness the decree, how I bring it back because
my husband says it doesn't fit, marriage made him too fat
to wear divorce at the pool this season. Nothing's urgent
anymore, except the children, the born and to be born.
Here's the sales slip and here's the box
it came in, this decree, with no mar but the one slit
to slide it in and out. Good luck with cracked decrees.
I'll tell my darlings that it's back where it belongs,
that we too shall be packed and gone soon, that the babies
will be stuffed like bunnies back in the hat for the trip.
I'll tell him that I walk in and the High Court looks
at my hands walking guard on my belly, thinks, one slip
and the woman wins. I win. The trap unlocks.

EXILE

xliii.
Burning burning burning burning
O Lord Thou pluckest me out

—T. S. Eliot

Labor, Columbus, All Souls, the world sects like a grapefruit
into her wedgy pulps: Alabama is too near the bulge
for comfort. And I'm so full of the dog latitude,
so pregnant I stop, there is no such place as pausing.
I stop inside, where it kicks: here's a multitude
of celebrants in the burning Grove squabbling to indulge
a whim for the exit. How I loved Musical Chairs.
Speed is its own revenge. O Lord let my baby passing
out hurt like the slow strafe of Fall, like his slow
choo-choos, like a spectacle of the slow Jews in hell.
My lips must burn, my meat from the bone must tear and pull.
I am Miss Ezekiel.
It's too soon, the southern season's a liar. Labor Day's so
tempting, so *communist*, it makes you feel
so one you want to work the damn thing out by the root.

EXILE

xliv.
Hamm: If you must hit me, hit me with the axe.

—Samuel Beckett

Ah goes out to da gahden, leans oan dirt, peels mah eyes
and sez, Lause, dis ticular cup ain sane
's you mus spec. Watch out for the old Jewess takes
the dog scrolls to Babylon.
She's to be trusted.
At the used-car lot last night's drunk husband eyes
the panel trucks, the breasting lights and wheels, talks
to me, he says, Honey, it's all between the Fords
and Chevrolets. It's Tishri, the seventh day I've lain
in ambush for the ghosts of dead
believers. It hurts. It's the woodwork for one, prone,
and for another it's the *rentedness* of the bed,
the garden, the monthly aphids sucking at the door
for the rent. I see now how to frame
my children, petaled twixt a mattress and the floor.

EXILE

xlv.
God bless the Commonwealth of Massachusetts!

—Leo Albert Reardon

He told me that old men turn back into porcelain
before they die and that was an oyster
trapped in his skull made him do it to me again.
I've looked in the attic, the cellar, and behind the walls
where he likes to go to build, but he's gone even from there.
With one suitcase, I guess a good book, and all the beer
from the icebox. Yes, I've grown for a Yankee lady far
too lush and sentimental. Lucy, or Christie, calls:
I'd thought it was over and he'd cast her
back like an old teacup. Well, kids, how can you be sure?
An optimist gone north I can tell
because he took his overshoes and my beaver coat.
He looks ahead, out of Indian summer into fields
of Massachusetts snow. God bless the bastard leaves
us all with pets, plans, children and another runic note:

EXILE

xlvi.
Let me make one thing perfectly clear.

—Richard Milhous Nixon

"Mah dahlin wyf, *partus virumque scio, (et) poesis
qui ultimum cano*, you must've posed. It's coming
as it must, *ex camera* and on the one track
eating its own perspective, shoving your husband back
into the tall silk chapeau. Monte Cristo is drumming
at the walls. Stone of course. He begs us boys
help him chew the way out. His way out
is ours in. A dark room walled with stone loaves
made sandwiches of our lives.
My son, tell him, life is as funny
as a feeder cow with scours: there's a farmer, a freezer
and a knife. What if it were backwards, the finger
flicked the shutter, posed flesh out of film, and *He,
The Finger,* made us run down grave to belly?
If so I may be back, your breadwinner, if so out."

EXILE

xlvii.
Now get you to my lady's chamber, and tell her, let her
paint an inch thick, to this favor she must come.

—Shakespeare

Are these the buttons that were my breasts? It's the eyes
in the closet open the hatbox and ask:
where d'ye keep the pecans I've sifted from the dog yard?
Things come back, holidays and husbands, nut pies
I'll squirrel in the winter butt, all for the hard
escape when we'll burn our horrible fat bridges.
He'll be back. I've his second note and the purple flowers:
orchis, he wrote, *for my Tuscaloosa fornix.*
Hang them in the hall closet, buss him as he enters
under the violent arch, the petals blown. Should I tell him?
I'm in love anew, this time with an Eldorado Cadillac,
or, you being gone, I played strip poker
and no one noticed I was naked at the teats and rigid.
He says, *I Shall Return!* With all my cozy tricks
I still should be mauve, unbuttoned, and very very thin.

EXILE

xlviii.

. . . the expensive delicate ship that must have seen
Something amazing, a boy falling out of the sky,
Had somewhere to get to and sailed calmly on.

—W. H. Auden

The Halloween mistral brings him back
to Alabama, slowly, on the trim black wings
of the Southern. Smoke and spoondrift in his feathers give back
the smell that frightened Stephen Daedalus, rocking
over the corpse of his mother. This gamin at the station sings
Milord, till he smiles at me and I ask,
does Rodina Federova still scare them, trick or treat?
Will he tell me, I've come home to the wrong place?
Rodina is in Iowa, undoing under the feet
of *her* black angel. Don't, he says, Halloween is walking
all our ghosts into the avenue to be face to face
with the children. What's wrong is the mask.
Life, he says, has undertaken our features, tried to run
our lips together, our legs. Keep closed the sack,
I tell my belly, or the kid will melt in the sun.

EXILE

xlix.
Love likes a gander, and adores a goose:

—Theodore Roethke

I have a husband, better left alone, he lives
close to the walls, his lips against the calendar like a mark
of the old moon, another month drooling into the ads:
WEO. Jesus saves. I have a son who gives
nothing but promise like the flowering crack
in a dam. I have inside me, just for luck,
a daughter swimming through the mildew, waiting birth.
It's All Souls' Day, there's a beast in the works, the clocks
are stalled an hour, back to the first war. I have leads
on a Red Cross truck will take us to the dressing stations
high on Mons Veneris. Out on the street the lads
clamor for it, Mother Dampness packing their wounds with earth.
This war is gamic how she feeds
on all my pretty soldiers afraid to screw in the dark.
I have the pains beginning. I have patience.

EXILE

1.

In the far South the sun of autumn is passing
Like Walt Whitman walking along a ruddy shore.

—Wallace Stevens

Young November, like the farrowing sow, spills her days
among the rooms of a let house. The new tenants want us out.
You move the stove, they said. Everyone has to see
what was under the stove, what the cats have left, where
the afterbirth dried to the floor. I have a few days
left to wait. Waiting for my baby to come out,
I stayed here too long. Complacencies closed up, you see,
so I must wait longer. A day. A week. There's nowhere
I would rather die in labor. Nowhere.
My husband had the renters wait in line outside the door,
gave out cigars, said he needed
baptismal records and all their fingerprints. It took more
than patience. It's the young the old sow eats.
The house, the line, the month proceeded
till he is by the river bidding the bird adieu like Keats.

61

EXILE

li.

In the first look of love men find their great disguises,
and collecting these rare pictures of himself was his life.

—Mona Van Duyn

Thanksgiving is coming, we've all grown fat
on this book. What with the walls trembling and the skies
after them, there's no room left
for the broken minarets to stand like familiar boys
at my breasts. *You* might die in a small Southern town
with the engines running, but we won't, who slouch past go,
our bags packed and good luck flowering down
on us her pretty toys.
You are not so simply pleased, you are never so
direct. My husband traces the blue lines in my breast:
hours, miles, to the nipple, and says it lies,
its circle never held; and, Lover, there are no permanent joys
in musical chairs. You, creator, like what he defies.
You think that beside the tower all women are flat
with want, that our milk curdles to your particular taste.

EXILE

lii.

Fancy the brain from hell
held out so long. Let go.

—John Berryman

Some of our dependents hang by their claws from the edge
of the truck. We buried the costumes under the books,
made a nest for the cats, let the others trail along behind.
Determinations fill the black spaces between the white lines
on the highway. The happy town burns its one bridge
behind us. Departure brings strange looks.
All hope we'll sleep in warm snow.
They wipe their lips and we smile
at the young man, imperially slight, and his woman,
ever late Southern and never rudely about anything. It rains mile
after mile like rice at the wedding's end.
As death wags we wag our last happy good-byes.
He says: perhaps they can forgive all those sweet lies.
She says: it hurts, it's ready, I might let go.
The glorious termites say, not here, not on the road,
                                    not here, never, no.

Pitt Poetry Series

COLOPHON

This book is set in Times Roman types, a design first cut for the London *Times*. Ironically, it has never enjoyed popularity as a newspaper face, but its classic design and favorable character count have made it perhaps the most versatile typeface in common use today for books and magazines. The Linotype cutting is used here, and the book was printed directly from the metal by Heritage Printers of Charlotte, North Carolina. After the initial printing, the type was destroyed. The book was designed by Gary Gore.